How To Overcome Temptation

Deal with the root than dealing with the fruit

DR CJ KUMAR

Made with ❤ on the Notion Press Platform

www.notionpress.com

Dedication

To the Young Generation,

This book is dedicated to you, the vibrant and courageous youth of our time. You stand at the crossroads of a world filled with unprecedented challenges and temptations, yet brimming with extraordinary potential for righteousness and godly impact.

I dedicate this work to your unwavering spirits, your passionate hearts, and your minds hungry for truth. You are the generation that the Apostle John might have had in mind when he wrote:

"I have written to you, young men, Because you are strong, and the word of God abides in you, And you have overcome the wicked one." (1 John 2:14, NKJV)

May this book serve as a beacon of hope and a practical guide as you navigate the complex moral landscape of your time. Let it remind you that you are not alone in your struggles, and that the power to overcome temptation lies within you through Christ

Contents

Preface

My beloved in Christ,

Glory to God in the highest and peace on earth. In this work, "How to Overcome Temptation," we embark on a journey to equip you with the spiritual tools necessary to confront and conquer the temptations that assail us in this modern age. As we delve into the wisdom of Scripture, our focus is clear: to deal with the root of temptation rather than merely addressing its fruit.

The Apostle James, in his profound insight, reveals to us the genesis of sin: *"But each one is tempted when he is drawn away by his own desires and enticed. Then, when desire has conceived, it gives birth to sin; and sin, when it is full-grown, brings forth death"* (James 1:14-15, NKJV). This passage illuminates the critical truth that temptation's power lies not in external circumstances, but in the desires of our own hearts.

Throughout this book, we will explore strategies to identify and uproot these desires, transforming our hearts and minds through the power of God's Word. As Paul exhorts, *"Do not be conformed to this world, but be transformed by the renewing of your mind"* (Romans 12:2, NKJV). This transformation is the key to overcoming temptation at its source.

We will learn to "put on the whole Armor of God" (Ephesians 6:11, NKJV), not as a mere defensive posture, but as an active engagement in spiritual warfare against the root causes of temptation. We will discover how to "walk in the Spirit," ensuring that we "shall not fulfil the lust of the flesh" (Galatians 5:16, NKJV). Our journey will take us beyond surface-level behavioural modifications to the deeper work of guarding our hearts, "for out of it spring the issues of life" (Proverbs 4:23, NKJV). We will explore practical ways to cultivate a heart that is fertile ground for righteousness and resistant to the seeds of temptation.

Ultimately, our goal is not merely to avoid sin, but to cultivate a deep, abiding relationship with Christ. For it is in Him that we find our true identity and the power to overcome. As John reminds us, *"He who is in you is greater than he who is in the world" (1 John 4:4, NKJV).*

As you read, may you be encouraged and equipped to deal with temptation at its root, transforming not just your actions, but your very desires. May you grow in the grace and knowledge of our Lord Jesus Christ.

By The Grace, Through The Faith, In The Hope
CJ Kumar

Acknowledgments

I am extremely grateful to the countless scholars, pastors, and teachers throughout history who have delved deep into the scriptural pattern of overcoming temptation. Their insights have immeasurably enriched the young generation understanding of this important aspect of the Christian Walk.

I particularly want to thank my local church for their unwavering support and fellowship. My heartfelt gratitude goes to my Sunday School teachers and pastors, whose guidance and profound teachings have been instrumental in shaping my spiritual journey. Your dedication to nurturing faith and character has moulded me into who I am today, and this work stands as an outcome of your investment of your time, efforts to sowing the Word of God in my life.

To the vibrant and inspiring youth of our church, you are truly the hope of our future. Your passionate pursuit of Christ and your boundless energy have been a constant source of inspiration as I researched and wrote this book. Your struggles, victories, and unwavering faith in the face of modern temptations have deeply informed and enriched this work.

ACKNOWLEDGMENTS

I am indebted to my family and friends who have stood by me, offering encouragement and wisdom throughout this writing process. Your prayers and support have been invaluable.

To all those who have shared their personal stories of triumph over temptation, your courage and honesty have added depth and authenticity to this work.

Above all, I give glory to God in the highest, the source of all wisdom and strength. It is His Word that lights our path and empowers us to overcome. May this book faithfully reflect the divine wisdom revealed in Scripture, serving as a practical guide for those seeking to live victorious lives in and through Christ.

May all who read these pages find hope, strength, and practical strategies to overcome temptation and draw closer to our Lord Jesus Christ.

By Him, Through Him, In Him, For Him, With Him,

CJ Kumar

1. The Source of Temptation

My beloved in the faith, I write to you with a heart full of love and concern, knowing the challenges you face in this present age. As everyone who also faced like you, I want to share with you the wisdom that comes from above, to equip you in your battle against temptation.

Fundamentals of Temptation

"No temptation has overtaken you except such as is common to man; but God is faithful, who will not allow you to be tempted beyond what you are able, but with the temptation will also make the way of escape, that you may be able to bear it." (1 Corinthians 10:13 NKJV)

This verse offers several important insights:

1. Temptation is universal: It's a common experience for all people, including Christians. Yes, Temptation is common in everyone's life but as the disciples of Christ we must overcome and we will overcome. So, it is important for us to learn to overcome temptation.

2. God's faithfulness: The verse assures believers that God is faithful in the midst of temptation.

3. Limited temptation: God doesn't allow temptations beyond what a person can handle.

4. Provision of escape: God provides a way to overcome each temptation.

5. Ability to endure: With God's help, we can bear and overcome temptations.

This verse emphasizes that while temptation is unavoidable at the same time it's not impossible for Christians. The ability to overcome temptation is central to living a Christian life, as it involves trusting in God's faithfulness and utilizing the means of escape, He provides. This process of overcoming helps in spiritual growth and in maintaining a strong faith.

Recognize the Source of Temptation

First, understand this crucial truth: God never tempts anyone to sin. As James, our brother in Christ, writes:

"Let no one say when he is tempted, 'I am tempted by God'; for God cannot be tempted by evil, nor does He Himself tempt anyone." (James 1:13, NKJV)

Rather, temptation springs from the desires of our own heart. James continues:

"But each one is tempted when he is drawn away by his own desires and enticed." (James 1:14, NKJV)

This indwelling sin, remnants of our old nature, wages war against our soul. Be vigilant, for our adversary the devil prowls like a roaring lion, seeking whom he may devour.

1.Insights of Tests and Temptations:

Tests (Trials): Tests are situations God allows or brings about to prove and strengthen faith, character, and obedience.

* *James 1:2-3 (NKJV): "My brethren, count it all joy when you fall into various trials, knowing that the testing of your faith produces patience."*

* *1 Peter 1:6-7 (NKJV): "In this you greatly rejoice, though now for a little while, if need be, you have been grieved by various trials, that the genuineness of your faith, being much more precious than gold that perishes, though it is tested by fire, may be found to praise, honor, and glory at the revelation of Jesus Christ."*

Temptations: Temptations are enticements to sin, often arising from one's own desires or external evil influences.

* *James 1:13-14 (NKJV): "Let no one say when he is tempted, 'I am tempted by God'; for God cannot be tempted by evil, nor does He Himself tempt anyone. But each one is tempted when he is drawn away by his own desires and enticed."*

* *1 Corinthians 10:13 (NKJV): "No temptation has overtaken you except such as is common to man; but God is faithful, who will not allow you to be tempted beyond*

what you are able, but with the temptation will also make the way of escape, that you may be able to bear it."

2. God Tests but Not Tempts:

a. God's Nature:

- James 1:13 (NKJV) clearly states: *"For God cannot be tempted by evil, nor does He Himself tempt anyone."*

- This aligns with God's holy and righteous nature, as described in *1 John 1:5 (NKJV): "God is light and in Him is no darkness at all."*

b. Purpose of Testing:

- Tests are meant to strengthen and prove faith.

- *Deuteronomy 8:2 (NKJV): "And you shall remember that the Lord your God led you all the way these forty years in the wilderness, to humble you and test you, to know what was in your heart, whether you would keep His commandments or not."*

c. Outcomes of Tests:

- *Romans 5:3-4 (NKJV): "And not only that, but we also glory in tribulations, knowing that tribulation produces perseverance; and perseverance, character; and character, hope."*

d. God's Faithfulness in Temptation:

1 Corinthians 10:13 assures that God provides a way of escape in temptations, showing His faithfulness even when allowing temptations.

The Bible clearly distinguishes between tests, which God uses for spiritual growth and strengthening of faith, and temptations, which lead to sin and do not originate from God. God's tests are always intended for good, to refine and strengthen believers, while temptations aim to lead one away from God. This distinction is crucial in understanding God's character and His interactions with believers.

Difference between Test and Temptation	
Test	**Temptation**
God tests	Satan tempts
Tests make us perfect in faith.	Temptations destroy faith.
Tests reveal Grace: *1 Peter 5:10 [AMP] After you have suffered for a little while, the God of all grace [who imparts His blessing and favor], who called you to His own eternal glory in Christ, will Himself complete, confirm, strengthen, and establish you [making you what you ought to be].*	Temptations reveal sinfulness
Tests set us up to succeed. *1 Peter 5:10 [AMP]*	Temptations set us up to fail.

Difference between Test and Temptation	
Test	**Temptation**
Tests prove strength by His Grace *2 Corinthians 12:9 And He said to me, "**My grace** is sufficient for you, for **My strength is made perfect in weakness**." Therefore most gladly I will rather boast in my infirmities, that the power of Christ may rest upon me.*	Temptations prove weakness, As if we are a failure As if we are weak As if we can not
Testing of our faith produces patience *James 1:2-3* *2 My brethren, count it all joy when you fall into various trials, 3 knowing that **the testing of your faith produces patience.****	Temptations produce sin and guilt.

So, what would save us from both Tests and Temptations?

OR

How to Overcome Tests and Temptations.

The answer is By Grace, Through Faith

Ephesians 2:8
For by grace you have been saved through faith, and that not of yourselves; it is the gift of God

That's the reason Jesus said to Peter,

*[Luke 22:31-32] 31 And the Lord said, "Simon, Simon! Indeed, Satan has asked for you, that he may sift you as wheat. 32 But I have prayed for you, that **your faith should not fail**; and when you have returned to Me, strengthen your brethren."*

And Jesus said to Paul,

*2 Corinthians 12:9 And He said to me, "**My grace** is sufficient for you, for **My strength is made perfect in weakness.**" Therefore most gladly I will rather boast in my infirmities, that the power of Christ may rest upon me.*

Do not get scared of Temptation but remember the THREE things:

First: *Romans 8:37 Yet in all these things **we are more than conquerors** through Him who loved us.*

Second: *1 John 4:4 You are of God, little children, and have overcome them, because **He who is in you is greater than he who is in the world.***

Third: *James 1:12 Blessed is the man who endures temptation; for when he has been approved, **he will receive the crown of life** which the Lord has promised to those who love Him.*

*Above all James says, consider it a great joy, my brothers and sisters, whenever you experience various trials, because you know that **the testing of your faith** produces endurance. And let endurance have its full effect, so that you may be **mature and complete, lacking nothing** (James 1:2–4).*

Now we understand the Source of the Temptation is not God but the Devil.

2. The Force of Temptation

Dear brothers and sisters of the young generation,

Grace and peace to you from God our Father and the Lord Jesus Christ. I write to you about a matter of utmost importance - the force of temptation that dwells within us all.

The temptation is a powerful force that can lead us astray if we do not understand its true nature. It is my deepest hope that by sharing these truths with you, you may be better equipped to resist temptation and live a life pleasing to God.

First, we must recognize the source of temptation. It does not come from God, for as James writes, *"Let no one say when he is tempted, 'I am tempted by God'; for God cannot be tempted by evil, nor does He Himself tempt anyone" (James 1:13, NKJV).* Rather, temptation arises from our own sinful desires. James continues, *"But each one is tempted when he is drawn away by his own desires and enticed" (James 1:14, NKJV).* The desires of the men are powerful and enticed (trap).

This truth may be difficult to accept, but it is crucial for our spiritual growth. We cannot blame external forces or circumstances for our temptations. The root of temptation lies within our own hearts. As the prophet Jeremiah declared, *"The heart is deceitful above all things, and desperately wicked; Who can know it?" (Jeremiah 17:9, NKJV)*.

Understanding this, we must be vigilant in guarding our hearts. Solomon, in his wisdom, instructed, *"Keep your heart with all diligence, for out of it spring the issues of life" (Proverbs 4:23, NKJV)*. Our hearts, left unchecked, can lead us into sin and destruction. And he also instructs us in *Proverbs 5:22-23 (NKJV) 22 His own iniquities entrap the wicked man, And he is caught in the cords of his sin. 23 He shall die for lack of instruction, And in the greatness of his folly he shall go astray.*

But take heart, my young friends, for though the force of temptation is strong, we are not left defenceless. The Lord has provided us with powerful weapons to combat these sinful desires. As the psalmist wrote, *"Your word I have hidden in my heart, that I might not sin against You" (Psalm 119:11, NKJV)*. Immerse yourselves in the Scriptures, for they are a shield against temptation.

Moreover, we must be aware of the deceptive nature of sin. It often appears attractive and harmless at first, but its consequences are terrible. As James warns, *"Then, when desire has conceived, it gives birth to sin; and sin, when it is full-grown, brings forth death" (James 1:15, NKJV)*. Do not be fooled by the temporary pleasures sin may offer, for they lead only to destruction.

I remind you of the hope we have in Christ. Though we may stumble, His grace is sufficient. As John wrote, *"My little children, these things I write to you, so that you may not sin. And if anyone sins, we have an Advocate with the Father, Jesus Christ the righteous" (1 John 2:1, NKJV)*.

May the Lord strengthen you and keep you from falling. May He grant you wisdom to discern the true nature of temptation and the courage to resist it. And may you grow in the grace and knowledge of our Lord and Savior Jesus Christ.

Now we understand the Force of the Temptation is within us that is our own sinful desire.

3. The Course of Temptation

To the beloved young believers of this generation, grace and peace to you from God our Father and the Lord Jesus Christ.

My beloved, let's address another matter of utmost importance "The Course of Temptation". For we know the struggles we face in this world of constant distractions and allurements. But take heart, for our Lord has overcome the world, and through Him, we too can overcome. *John 16: 33 These things I have spoken to you, that in Me you may have peace. In the world you will have tribulation; but be of good cheer, I have overcome the world.".*

Let us begin by examining the words of James, the servant of God and of the Lord Jesus Christ: *"But each one is tempted when he is drawn away by his own desires and enticed. **Then, when desire has conceived, it gives birth to sin; and sin, when it is full-grown, brings forth death"** (James 1:14-15, NKJV).*

Beloved, understand that temptation follows a course, much like a thorn that grows in a field of wheat. Left unchecked, it takes over, choking out the good fruit. This thorn of temptation has three distinct features: *a root, a shoot, and a fruit.*

The root of temptation is a selfish desire. ***The shoot*** is a sinful decision. And the resulting ***fruit*** is a sure defeat. This progression is as certain as the law of gravity, and we must be vigilant against it.

Let us first examine the root: a selfish desire. Not all desires are inherently sinful, for God has given us many good desires. But we must be wary of those selfish desires that crop up in our minds and hearts, seeking to lead us astray.

When these selfish desires meet with external temptations, sin is conceived. As it is written, *"For all that is in the world—the lust of the flesh, the lust of the eyes, and the pride of life—is not of the Father but is of the world" (1 John 2:16, NKJV).*

My young friends, when a selfish desire enters your mind, you must remove it immediately. For if you do not, it will, like a thorn, eventually choke you not to produce good fruit. *Luke 8:14 Now the ones that fell among thorns are those who, when they have heard, go out and are **choked** with cares, riches, and **pleasures of life**, and **bring no fruit to maturity**.* I urge you, to "bring every thought into captivity to the obedience of Christ"

2 Corinthians 10:5 casting down arguments and every high thing that exalts itself against the knowledge of God, bringing every thought into captivity to the obedience of Christ.

When such thoughts arise, immediately surrender your mind to Christ. Pray, saying, "Lord, my mind is Yours, and my heart is Yours. Please put Your thoughts in me." And if possible, open the Scriptures and feed on God's thoughts, for *"Your word I have hidden in my heart, That I might not sin against You" (Psalm 119:11, NKJV).*

Remember the words of our Lord Jesus when He was tempted in the wilderness. To every temptation, He responded, ***"It is written"*** (Matthew 4:4) ***"It is written again"*** (Matthew 4:7) ***"For it is written"*** (Matthew 4:10). We too must arm ourselves with the Word of God, for it is *"living and powerful, and sharper than any two-edged sword" (Hebrews 4:12, NKJV).*

Now, let us consider the shoot: a sinful decision. If left unchecked, the root of selfish desire will inevitably give way to the shoot of a sinful decision. Sin is the result of a selfish desire left unchecked and our deliberate choice to act on that desire.

As James wrote, this desire eventually "gives birth to sin." The Greek word for sin, ' hamartia' or 'hamartian'(266), means "to miss the mark." It describes an archer who aims at the target but misses the bull's-eye, a student who fails a test, or a person who knows the right standard of behaviour yet falls short.

Perhaps the most direct definition of sin is found in John's first epistle: "Sin is lawlessness" (1 John 3:4, NKJV). It is a deliberate choice to transgress God's perfect law, to go our own way rather than His way.

Beloved, we must be vigilant against these sinful decisions. *"Do not let sin reign in your mortal body, that you should obey it in its lusts" (Romans 6:12, NKJV).* Instead, we must "present [our] bodies a living sacrifice, holy, acceptable to God, which is [our] reasonable service" (Romans 12:1, NKJV).

Remember, young ones, that our battle is not against flesh and blood, but against the rulers, against the authorities, against the powers of this dark world and against the spiritual forces of evil in the heavenly realms (Ephesians 6:12). Therefore, we must put on the full Armor of God, that we may be able to stand against the wiles of the devil (Ephesians 6:11).

Finally, let us consider the fruit: a sure defeat. James warns us to look ahead to where our sin is leading us. As Paul said, *"The wages of sin is death" (Romans 6:23, NKJV).* This death is not merely physical, but can mean the death of dreams, relationships, ambitions, reputations, opportunities, and so much else that is good. The wages of sin kill our destiny. This is very purpose of devil, *The thief does not come except to steal, and to kill, and to destroy. (John 10:10 NKJV).* The devil tempts our desire to destroy our destiny.

In James's words, sin "brings forth death." This death signifies separation - separation from all that is good, and ultimately, separation from God. As it was in the garden of Eden, where Adam and Eve's sin led to their expulsion and separation from God, so it is with us when we give in to temptation.

My dear young believers, when we take the bait of temptation, we often fail to consider the consequences. Sin separates us from so much that is good and, all too often, results in the death of hopes, health, homes, and happiness. So how shall we deal with temptation, its cause, and its course? We must deal with it as we would deal with thorns in a field. It is not enough to cut off the tops of the thorns or to cut them down to the ground. These methods may make the field look good for a while, but the thorns will soon return.

No, we must deal with temptation at its root. We must allow God to pull out our sinful desires and replace them with godly ones. As David prayed, *"Create in me a clean heart, O God, And renew a steadfast spirit within me"* *(Psalm 51:10, NKJV).*

The spiritually victorious life is an exchanged life, not merely a changed life. We give God our old life, and He gives us a brand-new life. As Paul wrote to the Corinthians, *"Therefore, if anyone is in Christ, he is a new creation; old things have passed away; behold, all things have become new"* *(2 Corinthians 5:17, NKJV).*

Beloved, the battlefield is in the mind and heart. *"Set your mind on things above, not on things on the earth"* (Colossians 3:2, NKJV). And *"Finally, brethren, whatever things are true, whatever things are noble, whatever things are just, whatever things are pure, whatever things are lovely, whatever things are of good report, if there is any virtue and if there is anything praiseworthy—meditate on these things" (Philippians 4:8, NKJV).*

Allowing our minds to dwell on impure things is dangerous and damaging. These thoughts are the root of all sin. Therefore, guard your hearts and minds in Christ Jesus (Philippians 4:7).

Remember the words of that great reformer, Martin Luther, who said, "<u>You cannot keep birds from flying over your head but you can keep them from building a nest in your hair</u>." While you cannot prevent the devil from suggesting thoughts, you can choose not to dwell on them or act upon them.

Take heart, young ones, for our God is faithful. *"No temptation has overtaken you except such as is common to man; but God is faithful, who will not allow you to be tempted beyond what you are able, but with the temptation will also make the way of escape, that you may be able to bear it" (1 Corinthians 10:13, NKJV).*

When temptation comes, look for the way of escape that God has provided. It may be a change of environment, a word of Scripture brought to mind, or the presence of a fellow believer. Whatever it may be, God always provides a way out.

Stand firm in the faith, my young friends. Be on your guard; stand firm in the faith; be courageous; be strong. Do everything in love (1 Corinthians 16:13-14).

In closing, I urge you to put on the new self, created to be like God in true righteousness and holiness (Ephesians 4:24). Walk by the Spirit, and you will not gratify the desires of the flesh (Galatians 5:16).

Remember, young believers, that you are more than conquerors through Him who loved us (Romans 8:37). As Paul says, For I am convinced that neither death nor life, neither angels nor demons, neither the present nor the future, nor any powers, neither height nor depth, nor anything else in all creation, will be able to separate us from the love of God that is in Christ Jesus our Lord (Romans 8:38-39).

So now we understand,

The Source of Temptation	Devil
The Force of Temptation	Our own Desire
The Course of Temptation	Our Desire conceives and give birth to sin and Sin leads to death

4. Overcome Temptation: Source, Force and Course

Dear Beloved,

Let's recap as we continue to learn,

The Source: The Devil – Let's Resist him

The Force: Our own Heart's desire – Let's Guard our heart with the word of God, we are crucified and new creations in Christ

The Course: Our Desire conceives sin, leading to spiritual death – Let's learn to Flee from sin and Flee for our life!

Resist the source,

Guard from the Force

and Flee from the Course.

With this foundation, let us build further strategies to strengthen our souls against the wiles of the enemy.

The Source: The Devil - Resist him

Dear beloved young followers of Christ, As Paul instructed Timothy:

"Flee also youthful lusts; but pursue righteousness, faith, love, peace with those who call on the Lord out of a pure heart." (2 Timothy 2:22, NKJV)

Jesus said, *(Matthew 5:29-30 NKJV) 29 If your right eye causes you to sin, pluck it out and cast it from you; for it is more profitable for you that one of your members perish, than for your whole body to be cast into hell. 30 And if your right hand causes you to sin, cut it off and cast it from you; for it is more profitable for you that one of your members perish, than for your whole body to be cast into hell.*

This involves:

1. Avoiding situations that stir up temptation
2. Cutting off sources of temptation
3. Actively pursuing godliness

In these times of constant temptation and worldly allure, it is crucial that we arm ourselves with the weapons of our spiritual warfare. The enemy prowls like a roaring lion, seeking whom he may devour (1 Peter 5:8, NKJV). Therefore, let us be vigilant and steadfast in our faith, resisting the devil and drawing near to God. *"Resist the devil and he will flee from you. Draw near to God and He will draw near to you"* (James 4:7-8, NKJV). This, dear ones, is the key to overcoming temptation - active resistance coupled with fervent pursuit of our Lord.

Consider this truth: whatever you don't confront, you won't conquer. Whatever you don't resist has a right to remain. The tempter's suggestions and agents must not be tolerated in your life. ***Always stand up for what you believe in... Even if it means standing alone!*** You must stand firm, clothed in the full Armor of God, that you may be able to stand against the wiles of the devil (Ephesians 6:11, NKJV).

Remember, our struggle is not against flesh and blood, but against principalities, against powers, against the rulers of the darkness of this age, against spiritual hosts of wickedness in the heavenly places (Ephesians 6:12, NKJV). Therefore, take up the whole Armor of God, that you may be able to withstand in the evil day, and having done all, to stand (Ephesians 6:13, NKJV).

In your battle against temptation, understand the power and work of the Holy Spirit. As it is written, *"And the Holy Spirit helps us in our weakness. For we do not know what we should pray for as we ought, but the Spirit Himself makes intercession for us with groanings which cannot be uttered" (Romans 8:26, NKJV).*

The Holy Spirit is your ever-present help, your comforter, and your guide. He empowers you to resist temptation and live a life pleasing to God. As you yield to His leading, you will find strength beyond your own to overcome the desires of the flesh.

Remember this,

Proverbs 3:5-6
5 Trust in the Lord with all your heart, And lean not on your own understanding; 6 In all your ways acknowledge Him, And He shall direct your paths.

And

Isaiah 30:21 Your ears shall hear a word behind you, saying, "This is the way, walk in it," Whenever you turn to the right hand Or whenever you turn to the left.

Furthermore, consider this truth: *"Those who live according to the flesh set their minds on the things of the flesh, but those who live according to the Spirit, the things of the Spirit" (Romans 8:5, NKJV).* Your mind, dear ones, is the battleground. What you allow your thoughts to dwell upon will ultimately determine your actions.

Therefore, beloved, whatever things are true, whatever things are noble, whatever things are just, whatever things are pure, whatever things are lovely, whatever things are of good report, if there is any virtue and if there is anything praiseworthy—meditate on these things (Philippians 4:8, NKJV). By setting your mind on things above, not on things on the earth (Colossians 3:2, NKJV), you strengthen yourself against the attack of temptation.

In your struggle against sin, remember the words of our Lord Jesus: *"Ask, and it will be given to you; seek, and you will find; knock, and it will be opened to you. For everyone who asks receives, and he who seeks finds, and to him who knocks it will be opened"* (Matthew 7:7-8, NKJV). Persistence in prayer is a powerful weapon against temptation.

When faced with temptation, cry out to God. He is faithful and just to provide a way of escape. As it is written, *"No temptation has overtaken you except such as is common to man; but God is faithful, who will not allow you to be tempted beyond what you are able, but with the temptation will also make the way of escape, that you may be able to bear it"* (1 Corinthians 10:13, NKJV).

Beloved, in your battle against temptation, remember that you are not alone. Christ Himself was tempted in all points as we are, yet without sin (Hebrews 4:15, NKJV). He understands your struggles and intercedes for you at the right hand of the Father (Romans 8:34, NKJV).

Moreover, you have been given everything pertaining to life and godliness through the knowledge of Him who called us by glory and virtue (2 Peter 1:3, NKJV). You have within you the power to overcome, for greater is He who is in you than he who is in the world (1 John 4:4, NKJV).

Therefore, put on the Lord Jesus Christ, and make no provision for the flesh, to fulfil its lusts (Romans 13:14, NKJV). Walk in the Spirit, and you shall not fulfil the lust of the flesh (Galatians 5:16, NKJV).

Let us now consider practical steps to resist temptation:

*1. **Guard your heart:*** *"Keep your heart with all diligence, for out of it spring the issues of life" (Proverbs 4:23, NKJV).* Be careful what you allow into your mind through your eyes and ears.

*2. **Flee youthful lusts:*** *"Flee also youthful lusts; but pursue righteousness, faith, love, peace with those who call on the Lord out of a pure heart" (2 Timothy 2:22, NKJV).* Always, the best strategy is to run away from temptation.

*3. **Be filled with the Word:*** *"Your word I have hidden in my heart, that I might not sin against You" (Psalm 119:11, NKJV).* Memorize and meditate on Scripture to strengthen your mind against temptation.

*4. **Put on the full Armor of God:*** "Put on the whole Armor of God, that you may be able to stand against the wiles of the devil" (Ephesians 6:11, NKJV). Daily clothe yourself with truth, righteousness, the gospel of peace, faith, salvation, and the Word of God.

*5. **Practice self-control:*** *"But I discipline my body and bring it into subjection, lest, when I have preached to others, I myself should become disqualified" (1 Corinthians 9:27, NKJV).* Train yourself to say no to your flesh. ***"The art of leadership is saying no, not saying yes. It is very easy to say yes."***

Never say "YES" with your lips, if in your heart you are saying "NO"

6. *Focus on eternity:* *"For our light affliction, which is but for a moment, is working for us a far more exceeding and eternal weight of glory" (2 Corinthians 4:17, NKJV).* Keep your eyes fixed on the eternal rewards that await those who overcome. *(1 Corinthians 2:9 NJKV) But as it is written: "Eye has not seen, nor ear heard, Nor have entered into the heart of man The things which God has prepared for those who love Him."*

7. *Resist immediately:* *"Therefore submit to God. Resist the devil and he will flee from you" (James 4:7, NKJV).* Don't entertain temptation; resist it at its first appearance.

8. *Renew your mind:* *"And do not be conformed to this world, but be transformed by the renewing of your mind, that you may prove what is that good and acceptable and perfect will of God" (Romans 12:2, NKJV).* Continually align your thoughts with God's truth.

Remember, dear ones, that overcoming temptation is not about fighting up your own strength, but about relying on the power of God working in you. As it is written, *"I can do all things through Christ who strengthens me"* *(Philippians 4:13, NKJV).*

When temptation comes, recall the words of our Lord Jesus when He was tempted in the wilderness. To every temptation, He responded, "It is written" (Matthew 4:4, 7, 10, NKJV). Arm yourself with the sword of the Spirit, which is the word of God (Ephesians 6:17, NKJV).

Moreover, consider it pure joy when you face trials of many kinds, knowing that the testing of your faith produces perseverance (James 1:2-3, NKJV). Each victory over temptation strengthens your faith and draws you closer to God.

Beloved, do not grow weary in doing good, for in due season we shall reap if we do not lose heart (Galatians 6:9, NKJV). The battle against temptation is ongoing, but take heart, for Christ has overcome the world (John 16:33, NKJV).

Remember that you are not fighting for victory, but from victory. Christ has already conquered sin and death, and in Him, you are more than conquerors (Romans 8:37, NKJV).

Therefore, stand fast in the liberty by which Christ has made us free, and do not be entangled again with a yoke of bondage (Galatians 5:1, NKJV). You have been set free from the power of sin; now live as those who are alive to God in Christ Jesus (Romans 6:11, NKJV).

The Force: Heart's Desire - Guard Our Heart

Beloved in Christ,

The matter of utmost importance: the force of our own heart's desire and the critical need to guard our hearts. In this age of constant temptation and worldly allure, understanding and mastering this inner battleground is essential for every believer, especially you, the young generation.

Let us begin by acknowledging the powerful force that resides within each of us - our own heart's desire. The Scripture speaks plainly about this internal struggle:

"But each one is tempted when he is drawn away by his own desires and enticed." (James 1:14, NKJV)

This verse reveals a profound truth: the source of our temptations often lies within our own hearts. Our desires, when left unchecked, can become a formidable force pulling us away from God's path.

The apostle Paul, too, recognized this inner conflict:

"For the flesh lusts against the Spirit, and the Spirit against the flesh; and these are contrary to one another, so that you do not do the things that you wish." (Galatians 5:17, NKJV)

This war between flesh and Spirit is ongoing, making it crucial that we understand the battlefield - our own hearts.

Given the powerful force of our desires, the wisdom of Scripture exhorts us to be vigilant:

"Keep your heart with all diligence, for out of it spring the issues of life." (Proverbs 4:23, NKJV)

This counsel from Solomon is not mere suggestion, but a command for our spiritual well-being. But how do we practically guard our hearts in a world full of temptations?

As you resist temptation and guard your heart, be encouraged by these truths:

1. You are a new creation in Christ: *"Therefore, if anyone is in Christ, he is a new creation; old things have passed away; behold, all things have become new" (2 Corinthians 5:17, NKJV).*

2. You have the mind of Christ: *"For 'who has known the mind of the Lord that he may instruct Him?' But we have the mind of Christ" (1 Corinthians 2:16, NKJV).*

3. You are dead to sin: *"Likewise you also, reckon yourselves to be dead indeed to sin, but alive to God in Christ Jesus our Lord" (Romans 6:11, NKJV).*

4. You are more than a conqueror: *"Yet in all these things we are more than conquerors through Him who loved us" (Romans 8:37, NKJV).*

5. You have been given a spirit of power, love, and a sound mind: *"For God has not given us a spirit of fear, but of power and of love and of a sound mind"* (2 Timothy 1:7, NKJV).

6. You are complete in Christ: *"and you are complete in Him, who is the head of all principality and power"* (Colossians 2:10, NKJV).

Meditate on these truths daily, for they are your spiritual inheritance in Christ. Let them shape your identity and empower your resistance against temptation.

Furthermore, beloved, cultivate the fruit of the Spirit in your lives: *"But the fruit of the Spirit is love, joy, peace, longsuffering, kindness, goodness, faithfulness, gentleness, self-control. Against such there is no law"* (Galatians 5:22-23, NKJV). As you grow in these virtues, you will find yourself less susceptible to the allure of temptation.

"Let the word of Christ dwell in you richly in all wisdom, teaching and admonishing one another in psalms and hymns and spiritual songs, singing with grace in your hearts to the Lord" (Colossians 3:16, NKJV). Fill your mind and heart with songs of praise, and you will find strength to resist temptation.

Dear ones, as you face temptation, remember that your struggle is not unique. As it is written, *"No temptation has overtaken you except such as is common to man" (1 Corinthians 10:13, NKJV)*. Take comfort in knowing that countless believers before you have faced and overcome similar trials.

Moreover, consider the great cloud of witnesses surrounding you (Hebrews 12:1, NKJV). Draw inspiration from the faith of those who have gone before you, who through faith subdued kingdoms, worked righteousness, obtained promises, stopped the mouths of lions, quenched the violence of fire, escaped the edge of the sword, out of weakness were made strong, became valiant in battle, turned to flight the armies of the aliens (Hebrews 11:33-34, NKJV).

You too can overcome, for the same Spirit that raised Christ from the dead dwells in you (Romans 8:11, NKJV). Therefore, be strong in the Lord and in the power of His might (Ephesians 6:10, NKJV).

"Watch and pray, lest you enter into temptation. The spirit indeed is willing, but the flesh is weak" (Matthew 26:41, NKJV). Stay alert and prayerful, for the enemy never rests in his attempts to lead you astray.

"Be sober, be vigilant; because your adversary the devil walks about like a roaring lion, seeking whom he may devour. Resist him, steadfast in the faith, knowing that the same sufferings are experienced by your brotherhood in the world" (1 Peter 5:8-9, NKJV). Stand firm in your faith, knowing you are not alone in your struggles.

"For we do not wrestle against flesh and blood, but against principalities, against powers, against the rulers of the darkness of this age, against spiritual hosts of wickedness in the heavenly places" (Ephesians 6:12, NKJV). Remember the true nature of your battle and arm yourself accordingly.

7. Fix Your Eyes on Christ: Where we fix our gaze determines the direction of our hearts: *"looking unto Jesus, the author and finisher of our faith, who for the joy that was set before Him endured the cross, despising the shame, and has sat down at the right hand of the throne of God."* (Hebrews 12:2, NKJV)

By keeping our focus on Christ, we align our desires with His will.

8. Practice Discernment: We must be discerning about what we allow into our hearts: *"I will set nothing wicked before my eyes; I hate the work of those who fall away; It shall not cling to me."* (Psalm 101:3, NKJV)

This requires intentional choices about what we watch, read, and listen to.

9. Cultivate Godly Desires: As we guard against harmful desires, we must also cultivate godly ones: *"Delight yourself also in the Lord, And He shall give you the desires of your heart."* (Psalm 37:4, NKJV)

As we find our joy in the Lord, He shapes our desires to align with His will.

10. Rely on the Holy Spirit: We are not left to this task alone. The Holy Spirit empowers us: *"I say then: Walk in the Spirit, and you shall not fulfil the lust of the flesh." (Galatians 5:16, NKJV)*

By yielding to the Spirit's guidance, we find strength to overcome our fleshly desires.

11. Practice Self-Control: Guarding our hearts requires discipline: *"But also for this very reason, giving all diligence, add to your faith virtue, to virtue knowledge, to knowledge self-control, to self-control perseverance, to perseverance godliness." (2 Peter 1:5-6, NKJV)*

Self-control is a fruit of the Spirit (Galatians 5:23) that we must actively cultivate.

12. Guard Your Thought Life: Our thoughts shape our desires: *"Finally, brethren, whatever things are true, whatever things are noble, whatever things are just, whatever things are pure, whatever things are lovely, whatever things are of good report, if there is any virtue and if there is anything praiseworthy—meditate on these things." (Philippians 4:8, NKJV)*

By filling our minds with what is good and pure.

13. Pray for God's Protection: Jesus taught us to pray: *"And do not lead us into temptation, But deliver us from the evil one." (Matthew 6:13, NKJV)*

We must continually seek God's protection over our hearts.

Beloved, the force of our heart's desire is powerful, capable of leading us astray if left unchecked. But take heart, for we have been given all we need to guard our hearts effectively. As you navigate this world with its numerous temptations, remember the words of John:

*"For whatever is born of God overcomes the world. And this is the victory that has overcome the world—**our faith**." (1 John 5:4, NKJV)*

Finally, beloved, be encouraged. *"He who calls you is faithful, who also will do it" (1 Thessalonians 5:24, NKJV).* God is faithful to complete the good work He has begun in you (Philippians 1:6, NKJV).

Your faith in Christ is the ultimate guard for your heart. Nurture it, strengthen it, and let it guide your desires. For when our hearts are truly aligned with God's, we find not restriction, but freedom - the freedom to live as we were created to live, in full communion with our loving Father.

*"Now to Him who is able to **keep you from stumbling**, and to **present you faultless** before the presence of His glory with exceeding joy, to God our Savior, who alone is wise, be glory and majesty, dominion and power, both now and forever. Amen" (Jude 1:24-25, NKJV).*

May the Lord bless you and keep you, may He make His face shine upon you and be gracious to you, may He lift up His countenance upon you and give you peace (Numbers 6:24-26, NKJV). Stand firm in the faith, guard your hearts with all diligence, and may the grace of our Lord Jesus Christ be with you always.

The Course: Flee from the course

In this age of instant gratification and moral doctrine, you face trials unknown to generations past. Yet, the God who called you is faithful, and His Word remains a lamp unto your feet. Heed, therefore, these teachings, grounded in the eternal truths of Scripture.

My beloved in Christ,

Having laid the foundation of understanding temptation's source, force, and course, let us now delve deeper into the practical aspects of overcoming these trials. Remember always the summary of our previous discourse:

As Paul instructed Timothy:

"Flee also youthful lusts; but pursue righteousness, faith, love, peace with those who call on the Lord out of a pure heart." (2 Timothy 2:22, NKJV)

As we already seen, this involves:

1. Avoiding situations that stir up temptation
2. Cutting off sources of temptation (Matthew 5:29-30)
3. Actively pursuing godliness

The Course: From Desire to Sin and Sin to Death

Understand the dangerous progression of temptation. It begins with a desire, which, if entertained, conceives and gives birth to sin. If unchecked, this sin grows and ultimately leads to spiritual death. In your lives, this might look like a seemingly harmless flirtation that leads to sexual immorality, or a "small" compromise in integrity that spirals into a pattern of dishonesty.

How to Stop This Course:

1. ***Watch and Pray:*** Develop a habit of spiritual vigilance. Be aware of your weaknesses and the situations that tend to tempt you. Pray regularly for strength and wisdom to resist temptation.

2. ***Lift up the Shield of Faith:*** Remember that your faith in Christ is your defence against the enemy's attacks. When tempted, recall God's promises and the truth of His Word.

The Practice of Fleeing Temptation

Joseph, in his youthful days, provides an excellent example when he fled from Potiphar's wife (Genesis 39:12 NKJV).

In this age of instant access to all manner of temptations, be prepared to flee - to turn off the device, to leave the situation, to run from the very appearance of evil.

1 Thessalonians 5:22 [AMP] 22 Abstain from every form of evil [withdraw and keep away from it].

Now, let us advance in our understanding and application of God's wisdom.

Guard your mind and body in a world of compromised values:

"Flee sexual immorality. Every sin that a man does is outside the body, but he who commits sexual immorality sins against his own body." (1 Corinthians 6:18, NKJV)

1. Establish clear boundaries and accountability
2. Cultivate a biblical view of sexuality and marriage
3. Understand the meaning of fornication and adultery, both are sexual immorality.
4. Find freedom and healing in Christ from past wounds

My dear, as you implement these strategies, remember that your strength comes not from your own efforts, but from Christ who dwells within you. As you face the unique challenges of your generation, stand firm in the timeless truths of God's Word.

Now, let us delve deeper into the spiritual truths that will equip you to stand firm against the wiles of the enemy.

<u>1. *Understand the Enemy's Tactics*</u>

The adversary employs cunning strategies to derail your faith:

"Lest Satan should take advantage of us; for we are not ignorant of his devices." (2 Corinthians 2:11, NKJV)

- He steals the Word to prevent faith from taking root.
- He seeks to kill your faith, hindering salvation.
- His ultimate aim is to destroy your destiny and fruitfulness.

Satan is always on top of his work,

(John 10:10 NKJV) The thief does not come except to **steal, and to kill, and to destroy.**

Remember the parable of the Sower, where the enemy snatches away the seed, and how some fall away in times of temptation (Luke 8:11-15).

<u>2. *Recognize the Traps of Modern Philosophy*</u>

Be wary of worldly wisdom that contradicts God's truth:

"Beware lest anyone cheat you through philosophy and empty deceit, according to the tradition of men, according to the basic principles of the world, and not according to Christ." (Colossians 2:8, NKJV)

3. *Two prevalent traps to avoid:*

In these times, two great deceptions (Traps) threaten to lead you astray from the path of righteousness and eternal life.

Trap 1: The lie of "only one life to enjoy":

The first trap is the belief that there is only one life to live, and that it must be lived solely for earthly pleasure. This lie echoes the words of those who say, *"Let us eat and drink, for tomorrow we die!" (Isaiah 22:13).* But I implore you, do not be deceived. Our Lord Jesus Christ has promised us life eternal and everlasting, saying, "I am the way, the truth, and the life. No one comes to the Father except through Me" (John 14:6).

Remember, dear ones, that *"the wages of sin is death, but the gift of God is eternal life in Christ Jesus our Lord" (Romans 6:23).* This life we now live is but a vapor, a preparation for the everlasting life that awaits those who believe. As our Lord said, *"Most assuredly, I say to you, he who hears My word and believes in Him who sent Me has everlasting life, and shall not come into judgment, but has passed from death into life" (John 5:24).*

Trap 2: The deception that "all is created for our enjoyment":

The second trap is the notion that all things were created merely for our enjoyment, without restraint or wisdom. While it is true that God has richly blessed us with many good things, we must exercise discernment. *"All things are lawful for me, but not all things are helpful; all things are lawful for me, but not all things edify" (1 Corinthians 10:23).*

Recall the garden of Eden, where God provided abundance but also set boundaries for man's own good (Genesis 2:8-9). Similarly, we are called to choose wisely, for as it is written, *"I have set before you life and death, blessing and cursing; therefore choose life, that both you and your descendants may live" (Deuteronomy 30:19).*

To overcome these traps of temptations, I urge you to:

Fix your eyes on eternity: *"Set your mind on things above, not on things on the earth" (Colossians 3:2).* Let your actions be guided by the promise of eternal life, not fleeting pleasures.

Seek true knowledge of God: For *"this is eternal life, that they may know You, the only true God, and Jesus Christ whom You have sent" (John 17:3).* Immerse yourself in Scripture and prayer.

Exercise self-control: *"But I discipline my body and bring it into subjection, lest, when I have preached to others, I myself should become disqualified" (1 Corinthians 9:27).* Practice moderation in all things.

Build up the body of Christ: "Let each of us please his neighbour for his good, leading to edification" (Romans 15:2). Use your freedom to serve others, not spoil the flesh.

Trust in God's promises: Remember, *"My sheep hear My voice, and I know them, and they follow Me. And I give them eternal life, and they shall never perish; neither shall anyone snatch them out of My hand" (John 10:27-28).*

Beloved, stand firm against these deceptions. Your life in Christ is not limited to this world, but extends into eternity. Use the gifts God has given you wisely, always seeking to glorify Him. For in doing so, you will find true fulfilment and joy that surpasses all worldly pleasures.

4. Embrace the Reality of Eternal Life

Understand that your existence exceeds this earthly life:

"And this is eternal life, that they may know You, the only true God, and Jesus Christ whom You have sent." (John 17:3, NKJV)

- Everlasting life begins now, in believing Jesus Christ. (John 3:16)
- And it continues to eternal in know God the Father through Jesus Christ (John 17:3)
- It's not merely about duration, but quality of life in Him and through Him.

This perspective transforms how you face temptations and overcome the traps of temptation.

We have everlasting life and eternal life: Let's look in to this for better understanding.

Eternal Life:

The term "eternal life" in the Bible often refers to a quality of life that is divine in nature, not just an infinite duration. It emphasizes the kind of life that God has and shares with believers.

Key verses:

*John 6:54 Whoever eats My flesh and drinks My blood has **eternal life**, and I will raise him up at the last day.*

*John 6:68 But Simon Peter answered Him, "Lord, to whom shall we go? You have the words of **eternal life**. 69 Also we have come to believe and know that You are the Christ, the Son of the living God."*

*John 17:3 - "And this is **eternal life**, that they may know You, the only true God, and Jesus Christ whom You have sent."*

*1 John 5:11-12 - "And this is the testimony: that God has given us **eternal life**, and this life is in His Son. He who has the Son has life; he who does not have the Son of God does not have life."*

These verses suggest that **eternal life** is about knowing God the Father and relationship with God through Jesus Christ, which has no beginning and no ending.

Everlasting Life

"Everlasting life" is often used to emphasize the endless duration of the life given by God to believers.

Key verse:

*John 3:16 - "For God so loved the world that He gave His only begotten Son, that whoever **believes** in Him should not perish but have **everlasting life**."*

*John 6:27 Do not labor for the food which perishes, but for the food which endures to **everlasting life**, which the **Son of Man will give you**, because God the Father has set His seal on Him."*

*John 6:40 And this is the will of Him who sent Me, that everyone who **sees the Son and believes** in Him may have **everlasting life**; and I will raise him up at the last day."*

*John 6:47 Most assuredly, I say to you, he who **believes** in Me has **everlasting life***

"Eternal" can emphasize the quality and divine nature of the life.

"Everlasting" can emphasize its unending duration.

Both of these terms are used to describe something that lasts forever. However, 'eternal' indicates something that has no beginning and no end. It typically relates to abstract concepts or spiritual matters. 'Everlasting', though, is about something that has a beginning (i.e. believing in Jesus Christ) but never ends.

Let me expand on this with a more precise explanation:

In biblical usage, the same Greek word **(aiōnion (166))** is often used for both concepts, with the specific meaning determined by context. When applied to God, it means "eternal" (without beginning or end). When applied to the life believers receive, it means "everlasting" (with a beginning but no end).

This distinction helps us understand that while God is eternal (has always existed), the life He gives to believers is everlasting (begins at a point in time (i.e. believing Jesus Christ) and continues forever).

The life that believers receive through faith in Christ is both **qualitatively** different (partaking in God's own life) and **quantitatively** infinite (never-ending). The divine, unending life that God grants to those who believe in Jesus Christ. This life begins at the moment of faith and continues throughout eternity.

Eternal (Greek: aiōnion (166))

- Has no beginning and no end
- Often used to describe God's nature
- Relates to abstract or spiritual concepts

Everlasting (Greek: aiōnion (166))

- Has a beginning but no end
- Often used to describe the life believers receive through Christ

5. *Engage in Spiritual Warfare*

Recognize that your battle is not against flesh and blood:

"For we do not wrestle against flesh and blood, but against principalities, against powers, against the rulers of the darkness of this age, against spiritual hosts of wickedness in the heavenly places." (Ephesians 6:12, NKJV)

So,

- Be sober and vigilant against the roaring lion (1 Peter 5:8-9).
- Resist the devil, firm in your faith, and he will flee (James 4:7).
- Stand firm in the Lord's might, not your own strength.

6. *Utilize the Weapons of Spiritual Warfare*

Employ the divine arsenal at your disposal:

"For the weapons of our warfare are not carnal but mighty in God for pulling down strongholds, casting down arguments and every high thing that exalts itself against the knowledge of God, bringing every thought into captivity to the obedience of Christ." (2 Corinthians 10:4-5, NKJV)

- Put on the whole Armor of God (Ephesians 6:10-18).
- Use the sword of the Spirit, which is the Word of God.
- Above all, take up the shield of faith to defend from the arrows of temptation.

7. Cultivate a Life of Prayer and Watchfulness

Remain alert and prayerful in all circumstances:

"Watch and pray, lest you enter into temptation. The spirit indeed is willing, but the flesh is weak." (Matthew 26:41, NKJV)

- Pray always with all prayer and supplication in the Spirit (Ephesians 6:18).
- Be watchful with all perseverance.
- You are not alone in this battle.

8. Recognize the Conflict Between Flesh and Spirit

Understand the ongoing struggle within:

"For the flesh lusts against the Spirit, and the Spirit against the flesh; and these are contrary to one another, so that you do not do the things that you wish." (Galatians 5:17, NKJV)

- Acknowledge the weakness of the flesh.
- Rely on the Spirit's power to overcome fleshly desires.
- Walk in the Spirit to avoid fulfilling the lusts of the flesh.

9. Pursue Holiness with Reverent Fear

Strive for sanctification, knowing the seriousness of sin:

"Therefore, having these promises, beloved, let us cleanse ourselves from all filthiness of the flesh and spirit, perfecting holiness in the fear of God." (2 Corinthians 7:1, NKJV)

- Cultivate a healthy fear of the Lord.
- Actively cleanse yourself from all that defiles.
- Pursue holiness as a lifelong journey.

10. Rejoice in God's Faithfulness

Take heart in the unwavering faithfulness of your Heavenly Father:

"No temptation has overtaken you except such as is common to man; but God is faithful, who will not allow you to be tempted beyond what you are able, but with the temptation will also make the way of escape, that you may be able to bear it." (1 Corinthians 10:13, NKJV)

- Trust in God's perfect knowledge.
- Look for the way of escape He provides.
- Let His faithfulness be your anchor in the times of temptation.

Beloved, as you face the temptations of this age, remember that you are more than conquerors through Him who loved us. Stand firm in the faith, be strong in the Lord, and let your light shine before men, that they may see your good works and glorify your Father in heaven.

5. Temptation – A Spiritual Warfare

My dear young ones, The battle against temptation is violent, but the victory is assured in Christ. *"Watch, stand fast in the faith, be brave, be strong" (1 Corinthians 16:13 NKJV).*

Remember, you are more than conquerors through Him who loved us (Romans 8:37 NKJV). *"Now may the God of peace Himself sanctify you completely; and may your whole spirit, soul, and body be preserved blameless at the coming of our Lord Jesus Christ. He who calls you is faithful, who also will do it" (1 Thessalonians 5:23-24 NKJV).*

<u>1. Understanding the Nature of Temptation</u>

Let us recollect and understand the source, force, and course of temptation. As James, the servant of God, wisely instructs:

"Let no one say when he is tempted, 'I am tempted by God'; for God cannot be tempted by evil, nor does He Himself tempt anyone. But each one is tempted when he is drawn away by his own desires and enticed. Then, when desire has conceived, it gives birth to sin; and sin, when it is full-grown, brings forth death" (James 1:13-15 NKJV).

Recognize, my beloved, that while the devil may be the source, it is our own desires that give temptation its force. The course, if unchecked, leads from desire to sin, and ultimately to death.

My dear children, I have written these things to you that you may not sin. And if anyone sins, we have an Advocate with the Father, Jesus Christ the righteous (1 John 2:1 NKJV). Stand firm in the faith, be brave, be strong (1 Corinthians 16:13 NKJV).

As we continue our discourse on overcoming temptation, let us turn our attention to the example set by our Lord Jesus Christ, who was "in all points tempted as we are, yet without sin" (Hebrews 4:15 NKJV).

2. The Power of God's Word in Resisting Temptation

Our Lord's encounter with Satan in the wilderness provides us with a perfect model for overcoming temptation. As it is written:

"Then Jesus was led up by the Spirit into the wilderness to be tempted by the devil. And when He had fasted forty days and forty nights, afterward He was hungry. Now when the tempter came to Him, he said, 'If You are the Son of God, command that these stones become bread.' But He answered and said, 'It is written, "Man shall not live by bread alone, but by every word that proceeds from the mouth of God."' (Matthew 4:1-4 NKJV)

Notice, dear ones, how our Lord responded to each temptation with the powerful phrase, "It is written." Let this be your strategy as well. Arm yourselves with the Word of God, for it is "living and powerful, and sharper than any two-edged sword" (Hebrews 4:12 NKJV).

3. The Importance of Knowing Your Identity in Christ

Satan's first attack was to question Jesus' identity: "If You are the Son of God..." (Matthew 4:3 NKJV). Remember, beloved, that your identity is secure in Christ. As John writes, *"But as many as received Him, to them He gave the right to become children of God, to those who believe in His name" (John 1:12 NKJV)*. You need not prove your identity to the enemy or to the world. Rest secure in who you are in Christ.

4. The Necessity of Spiritual Nourishment

Our Lord's response, *"Man shall not live by bread alone, but by every word that proceeds from the mouth of God" (Matthew 4:4 NKJV)*, reminds us of the importance of spiritual nourishment. In this age of fast food and instant gratification, do not neglect the daily feeding of your soul with God's Word. For as it is written, *"All Scripture is given by inspiration of God, and is profitable for doctrine, for reproof, for correction, for instruction in righteousness, that the man of God may be complete, thoroughly equipped for every good work" (2 Timothy 3:16-17 NKJV)*.

<u>5. *The Call to Be Doers of the Word*</u>

It is not enough to merely know the Word, my dear. We must put it into practice. As James exhorts us, *"But be doers of the word, and not hearers only, deceiving yourselves" (James 1:22 NKJV)*. Our Lord Jesus not only knew the Scriptures but lived them out perfectly in the face of temptation.

<u>6. *The Importance of Discernment*</u>

Be aware, beloved, that even Satan can quote Scripture, as he did when tempting our Lord (Matthew 4:6 NKJV). *Therefore, who "received the word with all readiness, and searched the Scriptures daily to find out whether these things were so" (Acts 17:11 NKJV).* Cultivate discernment, testing everything against the full counsel of God's Word.

<u>7. *The Power of Knowing Scripture in Context*</u>

When Satan misused Scripture, our Lord responded, "It is written again" (Matthew 4:7 NKJV). This teaches us the importance of knowing not just isolated verses, but the full context and the entirety of God's Word. Study diligently, my beloved, "rightly dividing the word of truth" (2 Timothy 2:15 NKJV).

8. The Authority We Have in Christ

Our Lord's command, "Away with you, Satan!" (Matthew 4:10 NKJV) demonstrates the authority we have in Christ. As it is written, *"Therefore submit to God. Resist the devil and he will flee from you" (James 4:7 NKJV)*. Stand firm in this authority, grounded in your submission to God.

9. The Ongoing Nature of Spiritual Warfare

Be aware, beloved, that overcoming one temptation does not mean the end of spiritual warfare. As Luke records, the devil departed from Jesus "until an opportune time" (Luke 4:13 NKJV). Therefore, "Be sober, be vigilant; because your adversary the devil walks about like a roaring lion, seeking whom he may devour" (1 Peter 5:8 NKJV).

10. The Promise of God's Grace in Temptation

Take heart, my dear, for God has promised, *"No temptation has overtaken you except such as is common to man; but God is faithful, who will not allow you to be tempted beyond what you are able, but with the temptation will also make the way of escape, that you may be able to bear it" (1 Corinthians 10:13 NKJV)*. Look for this way of escape in every temptation.

11. The Importance of Spiritual Preparation

Our Lord faced His temptation after forty days of fasting and prayer. While we may not fast for forty days, we must prioritize spiritual disciplines that prepare us for the battles we face. As Paul exhorts, "Exercise yourself toward godliness" (1 Timothy 4:7 NKJV).

12. The Power of the Holy Spirit

Remember that Jesus was "led up by the Spirit into the wilderness" (Matthew 4:1 NKJV). We too must rely on the Holy Spirit's guidance and power. As it is written, "Walk in the Spirit, and you shall not fulfil the lust of the flesh" (Galatians 5:16 NKJV).

13. The Importance of Worshipping God Alone

When tempted with worldly power and glory, our Lord responded, *"You shall worship the Lord your God, and Him only you shall serve" (Matthew 4:10 NKJV)*. In this age of celebrity culture and self-promotion, remember that true fulfilment comes only from worshipping and serving God.

14. The Reality of Spiritual Refreshment after Trial

After the temptation, we read that "angels came and ministered to Him" (Matthew 4:11 NKJV). Be encouraged, beloved, that periods of spiritual refreshment often follow times of temptation. As James writes, *"Blessed is the man who endures temptation; for when he has been approved, he will receive the crown of life which the Lord has promised to those who love Him" (James 1:12 NKJV).*

15. The Importance of Community

While Jesus faced His temptation alone, He immediately afterward began to gather His disciples. We too need the support of fellow believers. As it is written, *"And let us consider one another in order to stir up love and good works, not forsaking the assembling of ourselves together, as is the manner of some, but exhorting one another, and so much the more as you see the Day approaching" (Hebrews 10:24-25 NKJV).*

16. The Ultimate Goal: Christlikeness

Remember, my dear, that in resisting temptation, our ultimate goal is to become more like Christ. As Paul writes, *"For whom He foreknew, He also predestined to be conformed to the image of His Son" (Romans 8:29 NKJV).* Let every victory over temptation be a step toward this glorious destiny.

6. Summary

1. Understanding Temptation

Let us begin by examining the nature of temptation as described in James 1:13-15 (NKJV):

"Let no one say when he is tempted, 'I am tempted by God'; for God cannot be tempted by evil, nor does He Himself tempt anyone. But each one is tempted when he is drawn away by his own desires and enticed. Then, when desire has conceived, it gives birth to sin; and sin, when it is full-grown, brings forth death."

This passage reveals the source, force, and course of temptation:

1A. Source: The Devil

The enemy of our souls is cunning and relentless in his attempts to lead us astray. In your daily lives, you face an onslaught of temptations through social media, peer pressure, and the general worldly culture that surrounds you. Recognize that behind these temptations lies the work of the devil, seeking to destroy your faith and relationship with God.

1B. Force: Heart's Desire for the Flesh

Young people, your hearts are filled with desires and passions. These are not inherently sinful, but they can become a force that pulls you towards temptation. The longing for acceptance, the desire for romantic relationships, the pursuit of success and recognition - all these can become avenues for temptation if not properly directed and controlled.

1C. Course: From Desire to Sin to Death

Understand the dangerous progression of temptation. It begins with a desire, which, if entertained, conceives and gives birth to sin. If unchecked, this sin grows and ultimately leads to spiritual death. In your lives, this might look like a seemingly harmless flirtation that leads to sexual immorality, or a "small" compromise in integrity that spirals into a pattern of dishonesty.

2. Practical Steps to Overcome Temptation

Now, let us examine practical ways to overcome temptation using the power of God's Word:

2A. "Get Behind Me, Satan"

When faced with temptation, follow the example of Jesus. In Matthew 4:10 and Luke 4:8, we see His response to Satan's temptations:

Matthew 4:10 (NKJV): *"Then Jesus said to him, 'Away with you, Satan! For it is written, 'You shall worship the Lord your God, and Him only you shall serve.'"*

Luke 4:8 (NKJV*): "And Jesus answered and said to him, 'Get behind Me, Satan! For it is written, 'You shall worship the Lord your God, and Him only you shall serve.'"*

Young friends, when temptation comes, verbally rebuke the enemy. Speak the Word of God aloud. However, be aware that simply saying these words may not immediately end the temptation. The enemy may leave for a time, only to return later.

In your daily lives, this might look like:

- When tempted to engage in gossip, declare, "Get behind me, Satan! I will speak only what is edifying."

- If lured towards pornography, proclaim, "Away with you, Satan! My body is a temple of the Holy Spirit."

- When tempted to cheat on an exam, assert, "Get behind me, Satan! I will honor God with integrity in all I do."

2B. Understand That Temptation Will Continue

Luke 4:13 (NKJV) tells us, *"Now when the devil had ended every temptation, he departed from Him until an opportune time."*

Young believers, be prepared for ongoing battles. Successfully resisting temptation once does not mean you'll never face it again. The enemy is patient and opportunistic.

In your lives, this means:

- After resisting the temptation to drink at one party, be prepared to face the same temptation at the next social gathering.

- If you've overcome the urge to lie to your parents once, don't be surprised when the temptation arises again in a different situation.

- Even if you've managed to control your anger in one instance, be ready to face that challenge repeatedly.

Stay vigilant, as 1 Peter 5:8-10 (NKJV) warns us:

"Be sober, be vigilant; because your adversary the devil walks about like a roaring lion, seeking whom he may devour. Resist him, steadfast in the faith, knowing that the same sufferings are experienced by your brotherhood in the world. But may the God of all grace, who called us to His eternal glory by Christ Jesus, after you have suffered a while, perfect, establish, strengthen, and settle you."

3. Recognizing and Resisting Subtle Temptations

3A. "If You Are a Son of God"

One of Satan's subtle tactics is to challenge your identity in Christ. He did this with Jesus, and he'll do it with you. Remember 1 John 2:16-17 (NKJV):

"For all that is in the world—the lust of the flesh, the lust of the eyes, and the pride of life—is not of the Father but is of the world. And the world is passing away, and the lust of it; but he who does the will of God abides forever."

The enemy may tempt you by saying, "If you're really a Christian, you should be able to..." or "A true child of God wouldn't struggle with..." Don't fall for this trap. Your identity in Christ is secure, not based on your performance or ability to resist temptation.

In your daily lives, this might manifest as:

- Pressure to prove your faith by engaging in extreme religious behaviors
- Temptation to compromise your values to fit in with non-believing friends
- Doubting your salvation because you struggle with certain sins

Remember, Jesus didn't give in to Satan's "if you are" challenges. He knew who He was and didn't need to prove it. Similarly, you don't need to prove your identity in Christ to anyone.

4. The Blessedness of Resisting Temptation

4A. Who is Blessed?

Psalms 1:1-2 (NKJV) provides a beautiful picture of the blessed life:

> *"Blessed is the man*
> *Who walks not in the counsel of the ungodly,*
> *Nor stands in the path of sinners,*
> *Nor sits in the seat of the scornful;*
> *But his delight is in the law of the Lord,*
> *And in His law he meditates day and night."*

Young believers, true blessing comes not from giving in to temptation, but from resisting it and delighting in God's Word. This passage highlights both what to avoid and what to pursue.

4B. What to Avoid:

Walking in the counsel of the ungodly: Be cautious about whose advice you follow. In this age of influencers and social media gurus, ensure that the voices you listen to align with God's Word.

Standing in the path of sinners: Be mindful of the company you keep and the places you frequent. Your environment can either strengthen or weaken your resolve against temptation.

Sitting in the seat of the disrespectful: Guard against developing a cynical or mocking attitude towards faith and godly living.

4C. What to Pursue:

Delight in God's law and his Grace: Cultivate a genuine love for God's Word. This isn't about legalistic rule-following, but about finding joy in God's instructions for life.

Meditate on it day and night: Make God's Word a constant companion. In this digital age, consider using Bible apps or setting reminders to reflect on Scripture throughout your day.

5. Dealing with the Flesh

5A. The Weakness of the Flesh

Our Lord Jesus recognized the weakness of the flesh. Consider His words in *Matthew 26:41 (NKJV): "Watch and pray, lest you enter into temptation. The spirit indeed is willing, but the flesh is weak."*

Young friends, your flesh – your natural, unspiritual self – is weak and prone to temptation. This is why Jesus teaches such radical measures in *Matthew 5:29-30 (NKJV) 29 If your right eye causes you to sin, pluck it out and cast it from you; for it is more profitable for you that one of your members perish, than for your whole body to be cast into hell. 30 And if your right hand causes you to sin, cut it off and cast it from you; for it is more profitable for you that one of your members perish, than for your whole body to be cast into hell.*

And also in *Matthew 18:8-9. 8 "If your hand or foot causes you to sin, cut it off and cast it from you. It is better for you to enter into life lame or maimed, rather than having two hands or two feet, to be cast into the everlasting fire. 9 And if your eye causes you to sin, pluck it out and cast it from you. It is better for you to enter into life with one eye, rather than having two eyes, to be cast into hell fire.*

While these verses are not to be taken literally, they emphasize the seriousness with which we should approach temptation.

Practical application for your lives:

- If certain things consistently lead you into temptation, get rid of that.

- If particular friendships pull you away from God, it may be necessary to distance yourself.

- If certain places or events always seem to lead to compromising situations, avoid them altogether.

Remember *Matthew 16:24 (NKJV): "Then Jesus said to His disciples, 'If anyone desires to come after Me, let him deny himself, and take up his cross, and follow Me.'"*

Denying yourself isn't easy, especially in a culture that promotes self-indulgence. But it's necessary for following Christ. This might mean:

- Choosing to serve others instead of always putting yourself first

- Practicing contentment instead of always seeking the latest gadgets or fashions

- Pursuing purity in your thoughts and actions, even when it's culturally unpopular

Beloved young believers, the journey of overcoming temptation is lifelong, but it is possible through Christ who strengthens you. Remember always that you are born of God, and therefore have the power to overcome. Abide in Christ and in His Word, for therein lies your victory.

As you face the unique challenges of your generation – the constant connectivity, the pressure to conform, the allure of instant gratification – hold fast to the timeless truths of God's Word. Let it be your guide, your comfort, and your strength.

Recall our summary:

Source	Devil	Resist the devil
Force	Heart's Desire for the flesh	We are crucified and we are new creation in Christ
Course	The course of temptation: Desire conceives and give birth to sin and Sin leads to death	How to stop this course: Watch and Pray and Lift up the shield of faith

May you grow in grace and in the knowledge of our Lord and Savior Jesus Christ. To Him be the glory both now and forever. Amen.

Epilogue

Dear beloved in Christ,

As we conclude this discourse on overcoming temptation, let us recapitulate the divine wisdom imparted to us through God's Holy Word. In these perilous times, where the allure of sin is ever-present, you must stand firm in your faith, equipped with the full Armor of God.

Remember always the source of your temptations. As James wisely instructs, *"Let no one say when he is tempted, 'I am tempted by God'; for God cannot be tempted by evil, nor does He Himself tempt anyone. But each one is tempted when he is drawn away by his own desires and enticed" (James 1:13-14, NKJV). Be vigilant, for the enemy of your souls prowls like a roaring lion, seeking whom he may devour (1 Peter 5:8).* Understand the deadly progression of sin, from desire to death, as James so clearly outlines: *"Then, when desire has conceived, it gives birth to sin; and sin, when it is full-grown, brings forth death" (James 1:15, NKJV).* Cut off this progression at its root, fleeing youthful lusts that war against your soul (2 Timothy 2:22).

In your battle against temptation, put on the whole Armor of God daily, that you may stand against the wiles of the devil (Ephesians 6:11).

Ephesians 6:10-18 (NKJV) The Whole Armor of God

10 Finally, my brethren, be strong in the Lord and in the power of His might. 11 Put on the whole Armor of God, that you may be able to stand against the wiles of the devil. 12 For we do not wrestle against flesh and blood, but against principalities, against powers, against the rulers of the darkness of this age, against spiritual hosts of wickedness in the heavenly places. 13 Therefore take up the whole Armor of God, that you may be able to withstand in the evil day, and having done all, to stand.

*14 Stand therefore, having girded your waist with truth, having put on the breastplate of righteousness, 15 and having shod your feet with the preparation of the gospel of peace; 16 **above all, taking the shield of faith** with which you will be able to quench all the fiery darts of the wicked one. 17 And take the helmet of salvation, and the sword of the Spirit, which is the word of God; 18 praying always with all prayer and supplication in the Spirit, being watchful to this end with all perseverance and supplication for all the saints.*

Let the Word of God dwell in you richly, renewing your mind, that you may discern the good and acceptable and perfect will of God. *Romans 12:2 (NKJV) 2 And do not be conformed to this world, but be transformed by the renewing of your mind, that you may prove what is that good and acceptable and perfect will of God.*

Walk in the Spirit, my beloved, and you shall not fulfil the lust of the flesh (Galatians 5:16). Guard your hearts with all diligence, for out of it spring the issues of life (Proverbs 4:23). Practice self-discipline, bringing your bodies into subjection (1 Corinthians 9:27).

Remember always your identity in Christ - you are new creations; old things have passed away (2 Corinthians 5:17).

Set your minds on things above, not on earthly things (Colossians 3:2). Trust in God's faithfulness, for He will not allow you to be tempted beyond what you are able to bear, but with the temptation will also make the way of escape (1 Corinthians 10:13). Persevere in faith, knowing that the testing of your faith produces patience (James 1:3). You are more than conquerors through Him who loved us (Romans 8:37).

Finally, my beloved, take heart in this truth: *"You are of God, little children, and have overcome them, because He who is in you is greater than he who is in the world" (1 John 4:4, NKJV).*

May the grace of our Lord Jesus Christ be with your spirit as you fight the good fight of faith. Stand firm in the liberty by which Christ has made you free. The God of peace will soon crush Satan under your feet.

Now to the King of the ages, immortal, invisible, the only God, be honor and glory forever and ever.

His Grace be with you all. Amen.

BIBLIOGRAPHY

1. Nelson's New King James Version
2. Dake's Annotated Reference Bible
3. Holman Christian Standard Bible (HCSB)
4. Amplified Bible (AMP)
5. New Living Translation (NLT)
6. Bible Gateway
7. The NKJV, Open Bible
8. NKJV, Minister's Bible
9. The Interlinear Hebrew-Greek-English Bible
10. Influential Mentors and Spiritual Guides: Personal communication and spiritual guidance from pastors, Sunday School teachers, Vacation Bible School instructors, and other church leaders and mentors